AF593267

MEGA MACHINES

picthall and gunzi

Created & produced by:
Picthall & Gunzi Limited
21A Widmore Road
Bromley
Kent BR1 1RW
United Kingdom

Written and edited by: Christiane Gunzi
Designer: Paul Calver
Editorial assistant: Maudie Gunzi
Heavy machinery consultant: Gary Boyd-Hope

Hardback ISBN **1-904618-98-7**

Reproduction in Singapore by Colourscan
Printed & bound in China by WKT Company Ltd

Picthall & Gunzi would particularly like to thank the following companies for the use of their images:
Bucyrus International, Inc.; Caterpillar Inc.; Komatsu Ltd.; Liebherr (manufacturer of the world's largest cranes); Nathan Kress from Kress Corporation; Terex; Tesmec USA, Inc.

Please note that every effort has been made to check the accuracy of the information contained in this book, and to credit the copyright holders correctly. Picthall & Gunzi apologise for any unintentional errors or omissions, and would be happy to include revisions to content and/or acknowledgments in subsequent editions of this book.

CONTENTS

GIANT EXCAVATORS

This is the biggest excavator in the world. It has a bucket at the front that is as big as a bus. The excavator is very tough so it can travel over rocks. The driver's cab is so big that there is also space for a computer, a fridge and a microwave!

Can you see some steps?

Mega load

This excavator is loading up one of the world's biggest dump trucks. It can load tonnes of earth and rocks very quickly.

Wow!

See how tiny these chidren are next to the big excavator!

Can you point to?
a rectangle
a diamond
a circle
O&K
Light
Cab
Door
Kitchen area
Steps
Tracks
NORTH AMERICAN
CONSTRUCTION GROUP
S4006
TEREX
RH 400

SCRAPERS

Machines called scrapers cut the top layer off the ground. They make it flat so that roads can be put on top. Scrapers need lots of power so they have two huge engines, one at the front and one at the back!

Can you point to?

a number | an air filter | a step

How many engines does a scraper have?

Two scrapers working together to make a new road

Big bowl

As the machine scrapes the ground, it collects earth in the bowl. When the bowl is full, the driver empties the earth out through the bottom and starts all over again.

ROCK SAWS

This amazing machine is the world's biggest rock saw. It has a huge wheel at the front with teeth that can cut through solid rock. There are two stabilizers to keep the saw steady.

Sharp teeth

The driver can make the wheel turn quickly or slowly. All round the wheel there are steel cutting teeth that saw into the ground as the wheel turns.

What job does this mega machine do?

Tracks

The rock saw crawls along on tracks. The driver controls the cutting wheel from a seat in the cab at the back of the machine.

SLAB CARRIERS

These machines carry big, heavy slabs of steel around the factory. Carriers are really strong. They move quickly and can load and unload themselves.

Can you point to?

some lights | a safety rail | some steps

Super steering

The cab has two steering wheels and the seat turns all the way round so the driver can drive forwards or backwards.

Straddle carrier

This machine is called a straddle carrier. It can pick up red-hot slabs of steel. The straddle carrier moves very fast. It has good brakes so it can stop quickly too.

A Straddle carrier picking up steel slabs

What do these machines carry?

Lifting piston

Wheel

Steps

LADLE CARRIERS

Ladle carriers are used in steel works. They pick up, carry and dump huge, heavy buckets. The buckets are called ladles, or slag pots. They carry hot liquid metal and ash. Each machine has big tyres to help it carry its load.

Slag pot

Hook

Melting metal

This ladle carrier is tipping out a pot full of boiling hot metal. It looks like the lava in a volcano!

Cradle

Where is the big slag pot?

Cosy cab

These machines load and unload themselves so the driver can stay in the cab.

Mega load

These carriers have big tyres like the ones on an aircraft. They can carry 500 tonnes!

MINING SHOVELS

Massive mining shovels like this one work in coal mines and quarries. They crawl along on their huge, wide tracks. Strong steel ropes pull the big bucket up and down as it picks up earth and moves it to another place.

All around

This amazing mining shov can turn all the way round It has a huge cab so that the driver can work easily.

Big bucket

This machine works quickly and it can hold 100 tonnes of earth in its bucket.

Can you see the bucket?

Wow!

See how tiny these children are next to the two mega machines!

BLASTHOLE DRILLS

This huge drill is used for drilling holes in quarries. The tall mast carries big rods that can drill a very long way into the ground. When the hole is deep enough, explosives are put inside. They explode and blow big chunks of rock out of the ground, ready to be collected.

Mega mast

Blasthole drills usually move along on tracks. But sometimes they are carried on trailers that have lots of wheels. When the drill is being moved from one place to another the mast has to lay down flat.

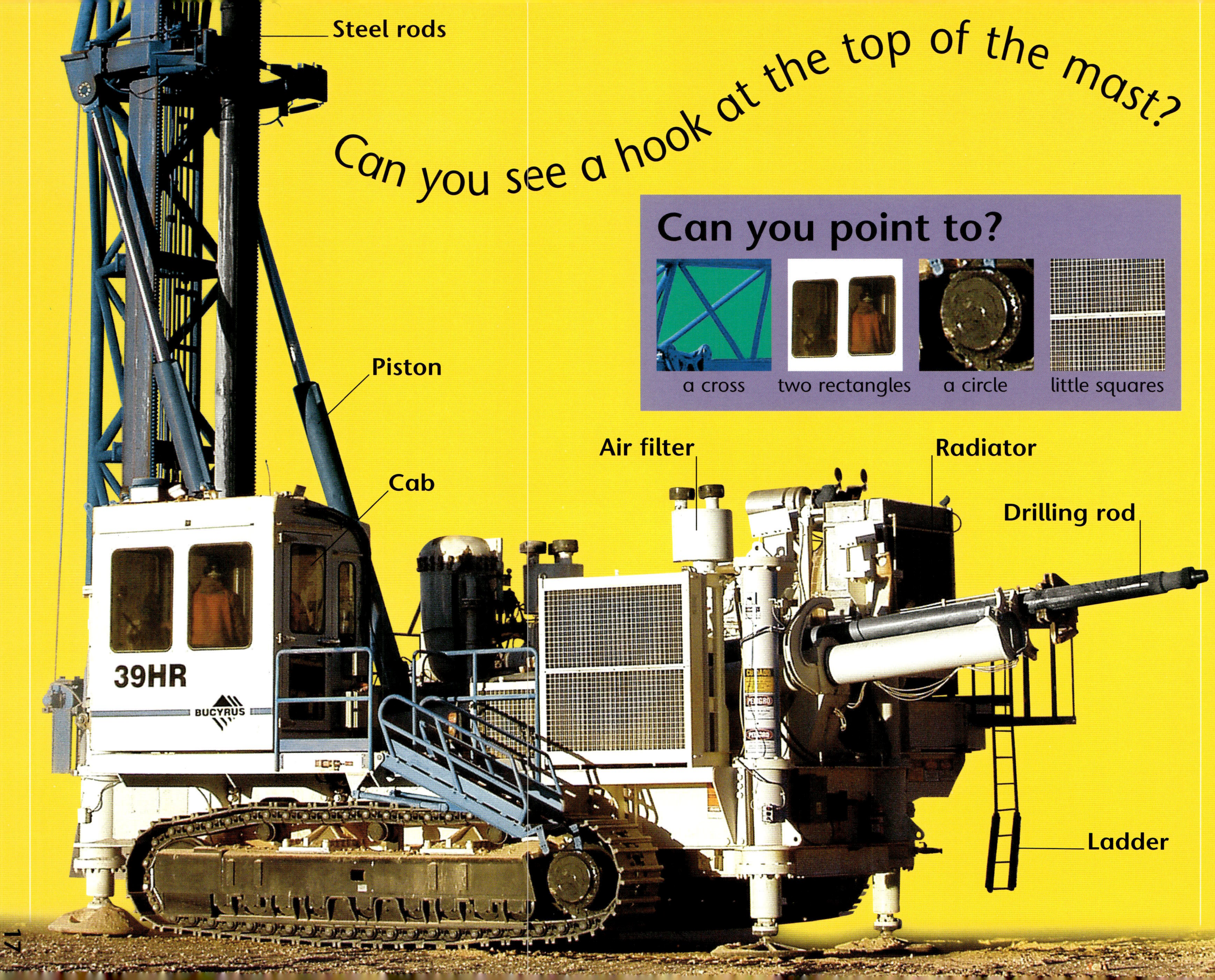

Can you see a hook at the top of the mast?

Can you point to?

a cross

two rectangles

a circle

little squares

COLD PLANERS

A cold planer is a special machine used for building roads and motorways. As it drives along it takes off all the old concrete and asphalt. This machine has four motors and they can work at two different speeds.

What does a cold planer do?

Keeping cool

The planer has a fan to keep it cool. The fan pulls air into the engine. Then all the exhaust fumes go out of the back of the machine, away from the driver.

Where is the conveyor?

Can you point to?

some chevrons

a light

some letters

Clever conveyor

The long bit on the front of the planer is called the conveyor. The rubble shoots out of the end and into a truck. When the job is finished the driver can fold the conveyor in half.

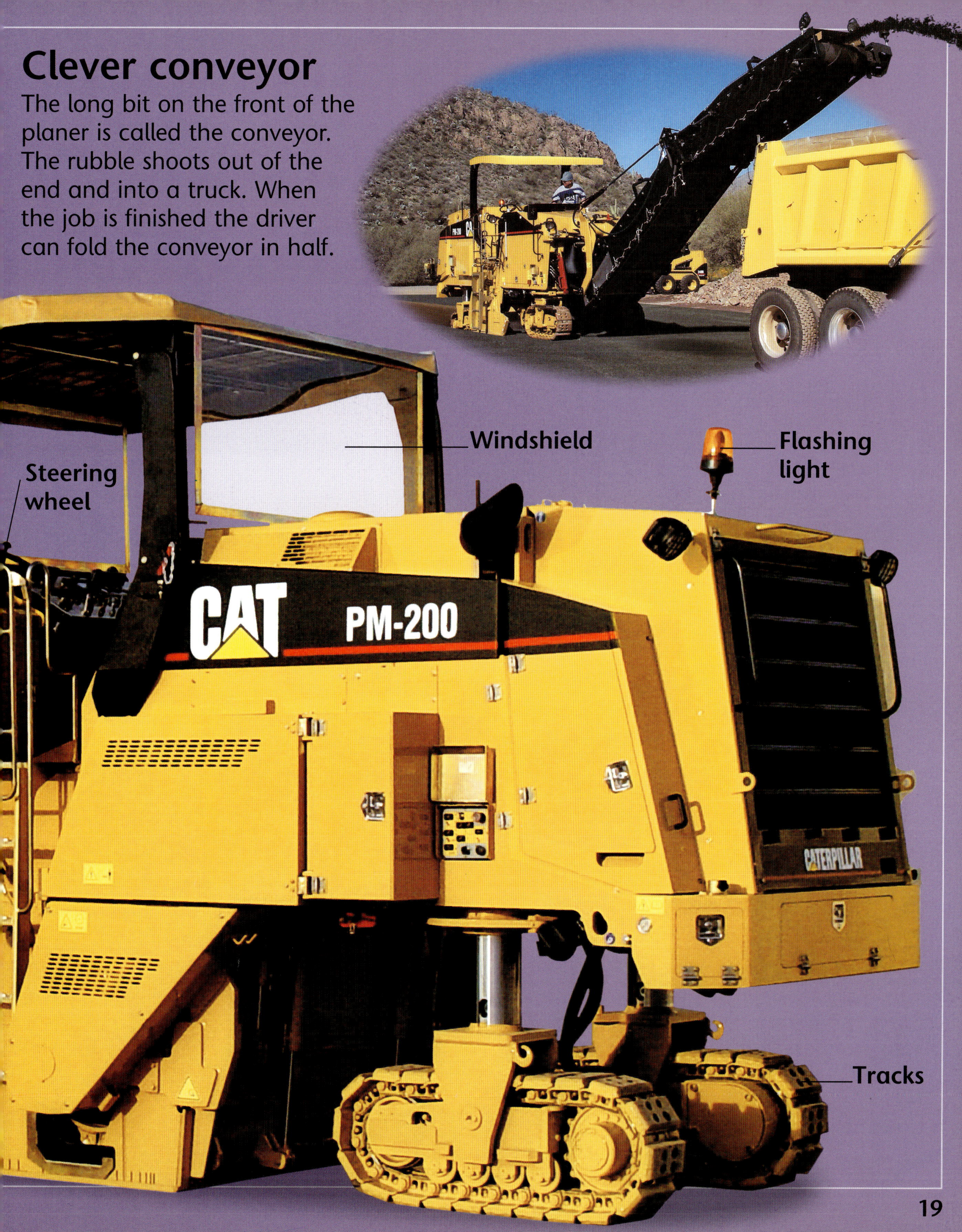

HUGE HAULERS

Haulers are used in coal mining. They carry coal from the mine to the place where it is stored. This big hauler has eight huge wheels to help it carry the weight. The driver dumps the coal out of the bottom of the truck. A canopy over the cab protects the driver in case any of the coal falls out.

Wow!

Can you see the two boys? They are three years old. See how tiny they are next to the mega hauler!

Canopy

Huge tough tyres

As big as a house

Haulers have to be enormous so that they can carry masses of coal. Some haulers are so big that you could fit a house inside their dump body!

SUPER DOZERS

The super dozer is one of the most powerful bulldozers in the world. It is so massive that when it is carried on a lorry it has to be taken in lots of pieces.

Can you point to?

a number

some tracks

some cables

How many lights can you see on this machine?

Mega blade

The driver controls the super dozer's massive blade from inside the cab. The blade can push, dig, carry and dump huge loads of earth and rocks.

Wow!

This little girl is three years old. See how tiny she is next to the super dozer!

DRAGLINES

This gigantic machine is called a dragline. It is used for getting earth and rock out of coal mines so that the coal can be dug out. A big bucket hangs off the front of the machine. The dragline swings out and drops the bucket. Then steel ropes drag the bucket along the ground and back up, filling it with earth on the way.

Super steel

Draglines need strong steel ropes so that they can work properly. These ropes connect to rope winders inside the machine. The winders are called drums. The driver controls the drums from inside the cab.

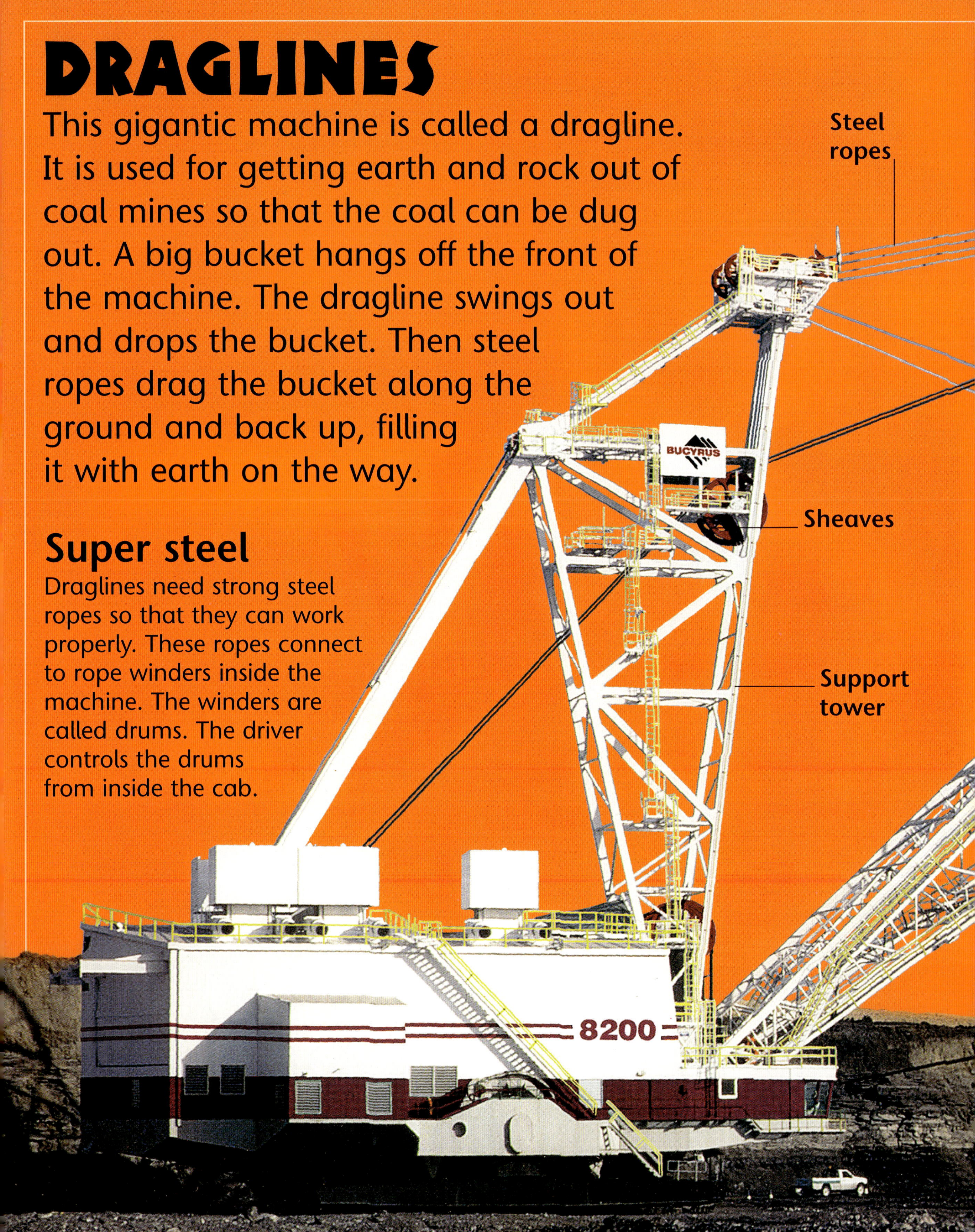

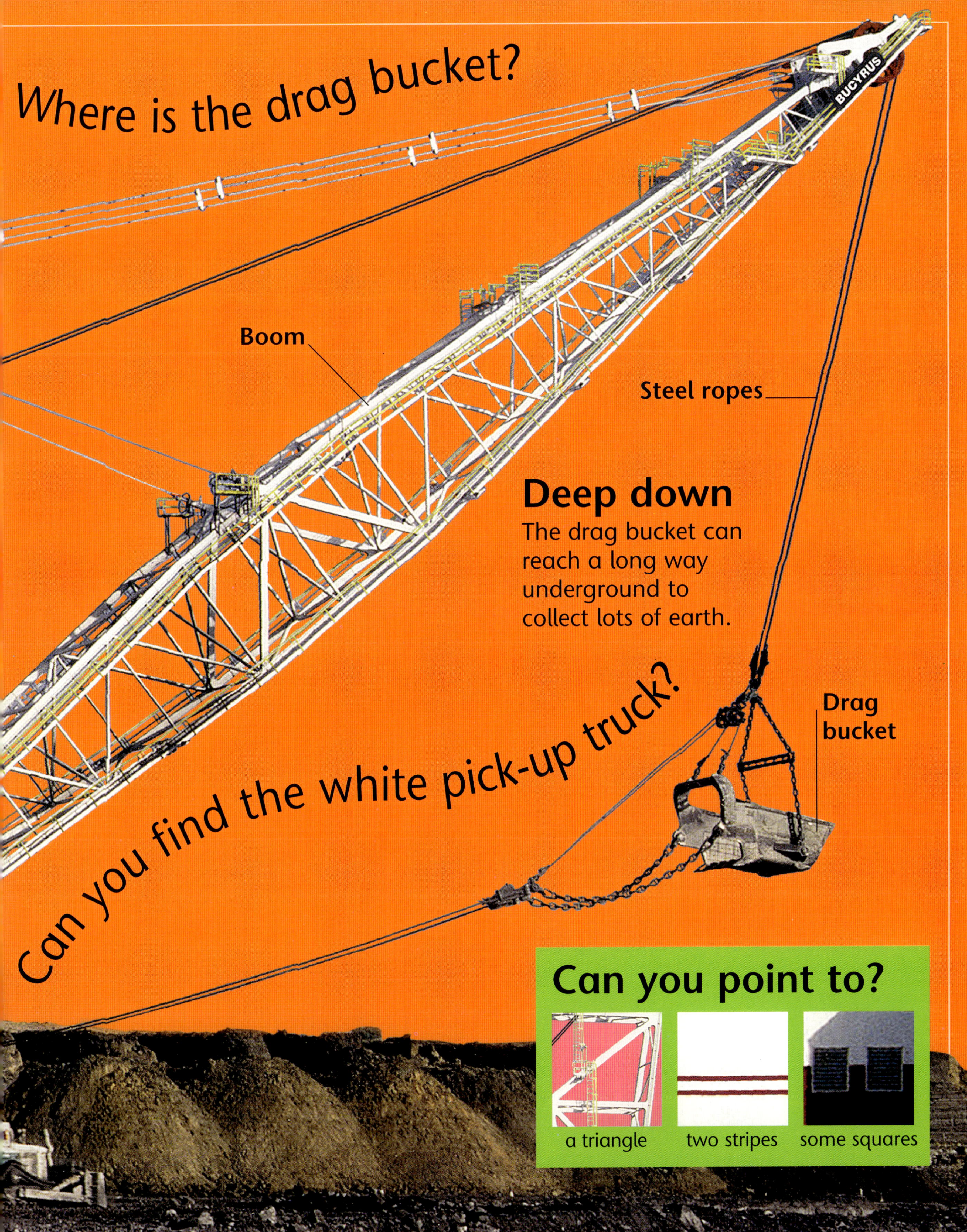

Where is the drag bucket?

Deep down

The drag bucket can reach a long way underground to collect lots of earth.

Can you find the white pick-up truck?

Can you point to?

a triangle

two stripes

some squares

TRENCHERS

A trencher is used for digging long, thin trenches in hard ground. It has a gigantic chainsaw on the front. All the rubble is carried along on a conveyor belt and shoots out of the back.

Can you point to?

some lights

a piston

a chainsaw

Mega chainsaw

At the front of the trencher there is a long chainsaw. It is very strong. Trenchers work in the same way as the chainsaws that are used for cutting down trees.

What do you think the stabilizers are for?

PIPE LAYERS

Special machines called pipe layers are used for putting long pipes into the ground. The pipes are so heavy that each machine has to have an extra weight on the opposite side to help it to balance and stop it falling over.

Standing tall

When a pipe layer moves along on its tracks the crane jib has to stay upright to help the machine to balance.

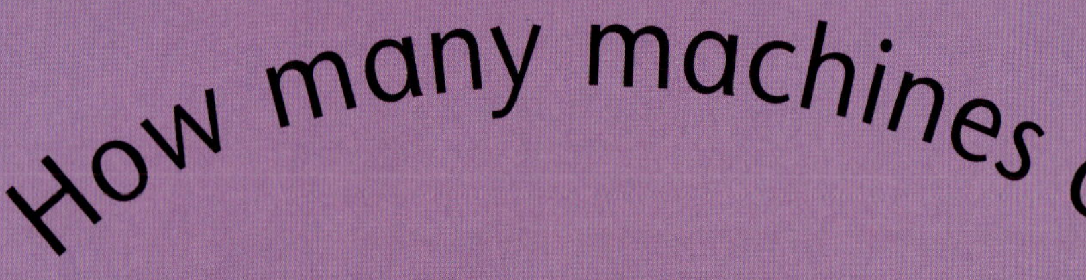

How many machines can you see?

Extra weight

Chevrons

Busy tractors

All these tractors are carrying one long, heavy oil pipe. They each have a crane jib attached on one side to help them to carry the pipe.

Up high

The machine is high above the ground so it cannot get stuck in the mud as it drives along on its wide tracks.